WANDERLUST WREN

The Ultimate Travel Guide To The Amalfi Coast Of Italy

Wine, Dine, and Unwind: How Anyone Can Effortlessly Explore the Budget-Friendly Wonders of Italy's Stunning Mediterranean Amalfi Coast

First edition

This book was professionally typeset on Reedsy.
Find out more at reedsy.com

Contents

INTRODUCTION

WELCOME TO THE ENCHANTING AMALFI COAST

A BRIEF OVERVIEW OF THE AMALFI COAST CHARM

Welcome to the magical Amalfi Coast, an oasis where blue waters meet craggy cliffs and history blends perfectly with spectacular beauty. This jewel tucked away along Italy's southwest coast is a mosaic of gorgeous scenery, quaint historical architecture, and lively regional culture. Get ready to be enthralled by the charm of charming towns perched on cliffs, the aroma of lemon orchards filling the air, and the rhythmic waves of the Tyrrhenian Sea resounding with stories from centuries past as you set out on this adventure with us.

This in-depth travel guide lets you explore the charm that marks the Amalfi Coast. The Amalfi Coast offers a unique experience for all types of travelers, whether experienced adventurers looking for undiscovered gems or first-time visitors looking for a picture-perfect getaway. Come along as we meander through the cobblestone streets of ancient towns, indulge in Mediterranean food, and discover the mysteries that make this seaside oasis an enduring travel destination.

In southern Italy, the Amalfi Coast stretches along the south edge of the Sorrentine Peninsula, and the island is considered a UNESCO World Heritage Site. Its striking scenery, with mountains plunging into blue waters, is a work of unmatched natural beauty. This introduction is your pass to explore all the region offers, from quaint settlements perched on cliffs to blue stretches reaching the horizon.

Let the sea wind lead you through a rich tapestry of experiences that meld perfectly with the way of life here. The enticing aromas of citrus fields, the calming beat of the sea, and the friendly hospitality of the locals create the perfect environment for a fantastic adventure.

WHY THE AMALFI COAST IS A MUST-VISIT FOR FIRST-TIME TRAVELERS

The Amalfi Coast is a celebration of life, love, and the enduring beauty of the Mediterranean—it is more than just a place to visit. This captivating coastline stretch will thrill your senses and create lasting vacation experiences, regardless of your interests in history, wildlife, or delicious food.

Come along with us as we explore the enchanted Amalfi Coast, where each cobblestone street has a tale to tell, each expansive vista is a work of art, and each instant is an opportunity to bask in the splendor of this idyllic seaside location.

CHAPTER 1: GETTING STARTED

PLANNING YOUR TRIP

BEST TIME TO VISIT

May and September are the ideal months to explore the Amalfi Coast. With temperatures between 20°C and 25°C, the weather is lovely, and there are many things to do without the crowds that July and August bring.

Smaller coastal communities close their restaurants and hotels for the same reason, even though November through March sees fewer visitors. Because of this, there are only so many hotel options outside of Naples and Sorrento. It is best to visit after Easter when the ferries and hydrofoils return because many do not operate during this time.

MONTH-BY-MONTH GUIDE FOR TRAVELING IN THE AMALFI COAST REGION

APR - MAY

The Amalfi Coast comes alive around Easter when the weather warms and businesses and hotels reopen after the winter hiatus. There are fewer people than during the summer since the citrus trees are blossoming, creating beautiful sights and scents. One of the greatest seasons to visit the area is spring.

Activities & Celebrations

The Ravello Concert Society presents concerts in various genres from April through October, with performances throughout the summer.

Ravello Concert Arena

JUN - AUG

The Amalfi Coast has its busiest months from June to August when several festivals and events occur all along the coast. Even though July and August are typically the most expensive, crowded, and hot months, they can also provide the widest selection of events, performances, and cultural activities.

Activities & Celebrations

The Ravello Concert Society presents concerts with various genres from April through October, with performances taking place throughout the summer.

The renowned Regatta of the Ancient Maritime Republics honors the history of the Amalfi Coast with colorful parades, historical sites, and, of course, the regatta. It takes place in June and is a favorite of the tourists.

Every year, in July, August, and September, Ravello presents a three-month-long arts festival with performances by numerous well-known musicians.

SEP - OCT

The best months to visit the Amalfi Coast are September and October. The weather is more peaceful and tranquil than it would be at the height of summer because it is slightly colder. Many services are still available, but fewer Italians travel there.

Activities & Celebrations

The Ravello Concert Society presents concerts with various genres from April through October, with performances taking place throughout the summer.

Every year, in July, August, and September, Ravello organizes a three-month-long arts festival that draws big names in dance, theater, and music.

Every year, Positano hosts the Festa del Pesce, where guests can savor delicious seafood while taking in parades and musical acts.

Positano

NOV - MAR

We discourage visiting the Amalfi Coast during the winter. There may be a lot of closed stores, eateries, and lodging facilities due to the potentially chilly and wet weather. While there are better times to enjoy the Amalfi Coast's splendor, some options will still be available in Naples and Sorrento, which make for enjoyable getaways over Christmas without the crowds.

DURATION OF STAY

SIX DAYS. Traveling to the Amalfi Coast requires effort, so it is best to take your time, unwind, and take it all in. There are lots of towns, beaches, and sites to see. If you will be here for five days or less, I recommend remaining put and making day trips to the nearby towns and beaches. If your trip is six days or longer, you can split up your time between visiting the Amalfi Coast and spending time on the island of Capri.

BUDGET CONSIDERATION

TRAVEL EXPENSES FOR AMALFI COAST

"How much should I spend on a trip to the Amalfi Coast?" is one of the most frequent queries tourists have. In actuality, the price of your vacation to this charming region of Italy will vary depending on many variables, such as your preferred mode of lodging, the things you do, and how long you stay.

Here is a summary of the primary costs to consider when planning a trip to the Amalfi Coast to help you get a ballpark estimate:

Lodging: There are numerous lodging choices along the Amalfi Coast to fit every budget. Depending on the location and season, a double room might cost anything from €80 to €300 per night. Budget-conscious travelers can find affordable hostels and guesthouses from €20 to €50 per night.

Food and Drink: Amalfi Coast dining can be pricey, especially in the more popular regions. A basic pizza or pasta dish will cost you between €10 and €15, but a three-course meal at a restaurant can cost you between €30 and €50 per person. For those on a tight budget, street food usually costs between €5 and €10.

Transportation: On the Amalfi Coast, transportation expenses can mount up rapidly. The most popular modes of transportation are buses and taxis, which cost between €20 and €60 for a taxi ride and €1.20 to €2.50 for a bus ticket. Car rentals are another option, although they may get pricey—the lowest rates start at €50 per day.

Activities: A few fun things around the Amalfi Coast are boat trips, hiking, and wine tasting. A boat tour will cost between €50 and €100 per person, a hiking tour between €15 and €30, and a wine tasting between €10 and €30. The price of different activities varies.

Travelers on a tight budget may spend as little as €50 per day to as much as €200 for luxury travelers to the Amalfi Coast. Take advantage of free activities like hiking and travel during the shoulder season (April- June or September- October) and select budget-friendly accommodations and meals to save costs.

ESSENTIAL TRAVEL TIPS

THINGS TO BRING FOR THE AMALFI COAST

While it can be exhilarating, packing for a trip to the Amalfi Coast can be difficult. Making sure you have everything you need for your vacation without sacrificing the lightness of the load is essential. Here is a packing list to help you prepare for your trip to the Amalfi Coast:

Lightweight Clothes: The summer months on the Amalfi Coast can be scorching. To stay relaxed and comfortable, bring clothing that is light and breathable.

Sunscreen: To save your skin from damaging UV rays, remember to bring sunscreen. If you intend to spend time at the beach, choose waterproof.

Please wear comfortable shoes: The Amalfi Coast is known for its slopes and steep staircases. Bring strolling shoes you can wear comfortably all day.

Swimsuit: Bring a swimsuit to enjoy the Mediterranean Sea's pristine waters. If you want to avoid bringing your own, you can rent chairs and umbrellas at the beach.

Day Pack: A pack must carry your camera, water bottle, snacks, and sunscreen regularly.

Light Jacket: To remain warm on the Amalfi Coast, bring a light jacket as the evenings can turn chilly.

Electrical Adapter: Remember to include an electrical adapter to charge your electronics.

Cash: You should carry some euros because tiny eateries and stores might only take some money.

Hat: When exploring the Amalfi Coast, carry a hat to shield your face from the sun.

Camera: The Amalfi Coast has breathtaking scenery, so you will want to take pictures at every turn. Remember to pack your camera so you can take some stunning images.

AMALFI COAST CUSTOMS AND ETIQUETTE

Visitors must comprehend Amalfi Coast customs and etiquette to prevent cultural misunderstandings. The following are some points to remember:

Dress Code: Since the Amalfi Coast is a stylish location, it is critical to wear appropriate clothing. It is customary to avoid wearing beachwear indoors and to avoid wearing revealing attire in places of worship.

Salutations: Kissing someone on both cheeks when you meet them is customary. Kissing is saved for close friends and family; it is appropriate to shake hands when meeting someone for the first time.

Tipping: Although not required, tipping is generous for staff in Italy. Tipping is typical in restaurants if you receive good service; a few euros are sufficient toward your tip.

Language: It is usually polite to learn a few essential Italian words, even if most visitors to tourist destinations speak English. Knowing some Italian shows that you are trying to observe local customs.

Respect for Religious Practices: Since there are many religious places around the Amalfi Coast, it is necessary to show respect for any practices related to religion. This respect entails not snapping pictures during services and dressing in an unrevealing attire when visiting places of worship.

Driving: Understanding the regional driving traditions is crucial for driving along the Amalfi Coast. Roads might be winding and narrow, so be prepared to go carefully on them. Furthermore, remember that parking can be tricky in busy places.

You can have a more pleasurable and courteous travel experience if you know and adhere to the Amalfi Coast customs and etiquette.

CHAPTER 2: ARRIVAL AND ACCOMMODATIONS

NAVIGATING NAPLES AIRPORT

TRANSPORTATION OPTIONS TO THE AMALFI COAST

Option One: Naples Central Station trains:

Advantages: Trains are cheap, available year-round, and allow you to avoid traffic.

Cons: There are none.

Two trains will take you to the Amalfi Coast from Naples Central Station.

The first is a metro train that goes directly to Vietri sul Mare and takes one hour. One of the more significant settlements along the Amalfi Coast is Vietri sul Mare. It is well known for producing handcrafted ceramics, and wall decorations made of ceramics are all over the town. The train costs €5.10 and takes approximately one hour.

Take note! The station beneath the principal station, Piazza Garibaldi in Napoli, is where the metropolitan train departs. (It could be unclear.)

To find it, navigate Naples Central Station's signage for Metro Linea 2. Tickets can be purchased online or at the station's electronic Trenitalia ticket booths. Remember to select Napoli Piazza Garibaldi as your departure station while conducting online searches.

Alternatively, you can go directly to Salerno from Naples Central Station (Napoli Centrale) by train. A major transportation center for the Amalfi Coast is Salerno, a tiny city located south of Naples. The train costs between €10 and €20 and takes less than 40 minutes. Purchase your tickets on the Internet. You can take a bus or a ferry from Salerno to the town of your choice along the Amalfi Coast.

Option 2: Boats departing from Naples Harbor:

Advantages: Coastal vistas, the easiest path from Naples to Amalfi and Positano

Cons: A more costly option that is not available during the off-season.

Direct boats from Naples to Amalfi and Positano are available if you visit between May and October. The boat line services are available from two different companies: NLG and Alilauro. Amalfi can be reached in roughly 90 minutes, whereas Positano takes approximately two hours. The port of departure is Molo Beverello, and one-way tickets range in price from €25 to €35. We recommend checking the ferry operator's websites to see which routes are running if there is rain or wind.

Option 3: From Naples Capodichino Airport, take a direct bus:

Advantages: Cheap, easy route straight from the airport

Cons: Traffic

There is a dependable bus from the airport to Salerno, even though we do not advise taking one from downtown Naples to the Amalfi Coast. Although few buses operate daily, it is a viable choice if your airplane arrival time coincides with the bus schedule. It takes around 90 minutes, and tickets cost €5.10. Once you leave at the Concordia station in Salerno, you can take a bus or ferry to your destination.

TIPS FOR SMOOTH TRAVEL

AHEAD-OF-TIME PLANNING FOSTERS EXCITEMENT AND ANTICIPATION

Having the dates of your trip planned out is exciting, especially if you are going somewhere as gorgeous as the Amalfi Coast. Plan your vacation arrangements with the thrill and anticipation in mind to give yourself something extra to look forward to and relieve some extra tension. If you could start the journey early by doing more research, why wait for all the excitement of the trip when you are there?

IMPROVABLE AVAILABILITY AND OFFERS

You may reserve a more fantastic selection of flights, lodging, and activities if you make your plans in advance. Early bird discounts are available, so you can save money and free up funds for other activities.

LESS TENDER LATE-NIGHT STRESS

As you rush to find available reservations, lodging, and transportation, last-minute planning frequently results in tension and anxiety. By organizing ahead of time, you may reduce the stress of making snap decisions and have more time to investigate and select the solutions that best suit your needs and financial situation.

PROTECTING FAMOUS ATTRACTIONS

Specific tours, events, and tourist sites have limited seats and can fill up rapidly, particularly in the busiest times of the year. By planning, you can guarantee you will be able to catch top picks by securing tickets and reservations for those must-see locations.

FORMING A COMPLETE GUIDELINE

A well-planned schedule that maximizes your time and guarantees you see all the sites and things you want to know when you start planning ahead of time. Advanced planning keeps you from feeling overburdened and missing stuff while traveling.

PACKING SMARTLY

When you pack quickly, it can be a significant source of stress. You can ensure you have everything you need and lower your chance of forgetting anything by organizing your belongings properly and creating a packing list in advance.

OVERVIEW OF POPULAR TOWNS (POSITANO, AMALFI, RAVELLO, CAPRI)

AMALFI TOWN:

The center of the Amalfi Coast, Amalfi Town, is a quaint beach town that is a fantastic starting point for exploring the surrounding area. Numerous excellent sights are easily accessible from the city, and there are many eateries, stores, and cafes to enjoy.

Amalfi Town, Italy

POSITANO:

Positano is one of the most visited villages along the Amalfi Coast, renowned for its breathtaking cliffside setting. There are many upscale lodging options, shops, and eateries, and the vibrant architecture and winding lanes are sure to wow.

Positano, Italy

RAVELLO:

Ravello is a serene village with lovely gardens and breathtaking vistas high in the hills above the ocean. Additionally, there are many cultural sites, such as the well-known Villa Cimbrone and Villa.

Ravello, Italy

PRAIANO:

Nestled between Positano and Amalfi, Praiano has a more sedate vibe than its more well-known neighbors. The town is a fantastic option for anyone searching for a more laid-back holiday because of its gorgeous beaches and environment.

CAPRI:

Capri, a famous island in numerous movies and literature, has two personalities: day trippers govern the island during the day, but locals and guests arrive at night to participate in a quaint custom. The Piazza starts at Bar Al Piccolo, where people congregate for an aperitif and, more crucially, to people-watch. Tasty dinners consist of freshly cooked seafood and handmade pasta; Aurora and Da Paolino are popular table choices.

Many insiders spend the day hiding in their hotels or on a premium lounger at Il Riccio or La Fontelina beach clubs. Hiking pathways encircle the picturesque village of Anacapri on the island's western side. The art-filled Villa San Michele and a shopping trip down the Via Camerelle, Via V. Emanuele, and Via Le Botteghe are noticeable.

Capri, Italy

MAIORI:

Maiori is a busy town with a large stretch of sandy beach at the eastern extremity of the Amalfi Coast. In addition to the easy access to some of the best sites in the area, there are lots of shops and restaurants to explore.

ACCOMMODATION OPTIONS FOR VARIOUS BUDGETS

THE AMALFI COAST

Amalfi and Positano are two of the most well-known coastal villages; nevertheless, Amalfi offers more reasonably priced lodging and restaurants than Positano. Amalfi, which lies in the coast's center, makes a handy starting point for seeing other local villages.

In the past, Amalfi Town was a solid maritime republic important to medieval trade. A prominent attraction is the Duomo di Sant'Andrea, a magnificent church that dates back to the ninth century known for its elaborate mosaics and spectacular staircase.

The center of Amalfi Town is Piazza del Duomo, the central square. It is a busy center encircled by eateries, stores, and cafes.

Best places to stay in Amalfi Town:
   Luxury: Anantara Convento di Amalfi Grand Hotel
   Mid-range: Hotel Marina Riviera
   Budget: Holidays Baia D'Amalfi

SORRENTO:

There are many different lodging alternatives available in Sorrento. If you visit Sorrento during the off-peak season or make early reservations, you might find more economical options than in other Amalfi Coast cities.

With its well-connected transportation system, Sorrento is an ideal starting point for seeing the Amalfi Coast. Positano, Amalfi, and Ravello are conveniently accessible from the town via bus and train, negating the need for pricey private transportation.

Because of its central location, Sorrento makes daily visits to Pompeii, Herculaneum, and Naples simple.

Sorrento is renowned for its magnificently beautiful surroundings. The village offers breathtaking sweeping views of cliffs overlooking the ocean.

Top hotels along Sorrento's Amalfi Coast:
  Luxury: Grand Hotel La Favorita
  Mid-range: Imperial Hotel Tramontano
  Budget: Hotel Tasso Suites & Spa

RAVELLO

The charming village of Ravello is atop a hill. It is well-known for its breathtaking views of the Mediterranean and enchanting scenery, including lovely gardens and secluded residences.

Cimbrone, a medieval mansion with exquisite grounds and breathtaking vistas, is one of Ravello's top attractions. The gardens are ideal for a stroll because the gardens contain statues, fountains, and vibrant flowers.

Best places to stay in Amalfi Coast in Ravello:
  Luxury: Caruso, A Belmond Hotel, Amalfi Coast
  Mid-range: Casa Vacanze Vittoria

Budget: Hotel Toro

SALERNO

Along with Sorrento and Naples, Salerno is one of the region's significant transportation hubs. Salerno is the end station for trains from larger cities, from which passengers can go by bus or boat to nearby coastal towns and villages.

The easternmost point of the Amalfi Coast is home to Salerno. It is well-known for having less expensive lodging and food options than nearby towns, making it one of the most incredible places to stay in the area on a tight budget.

Best places to stay in Amalfi Coast in Salerno:
Luxury: Hotel Montestella
Mid-range: Relais Vittorio Veneto – Luxotel & Apartotel
Budget: Hotel Plaza

ATRANI

Tucked between Amalfi and Minori is the charming little village of Atrani. You may easily visit Amalfi's attractions while staying in the more sedate atmosphere of Atrani because it is conveniently situated only a short stroll from the larger town of Amalfi.

Narrow lanes, traditional homes, and a quaint, cozy ambiance define Atrani's historic core. The town provides a window into the past and has much of its medieval beauty intact.

Best places to stay in Atrani:
Luxury: Palazzo Ferraioli – Hotel & Wellness
Mid-range: Flora
Budget: Hotel L'Argine Fiorito

RECOMMENDED BOOKING PLATFORMS

Booking.com: The most extensive selection of lodging alternatives is on Booking.com, which offers hotels, bed and breakfasts, apartments, and agriturismos. Great discounts and generous cancellation policies make this our preferred website for lodging in Italy.

Plum Guide: Visit Plum Guide if you are overwhelmed by the variety of Airbnb options; they have done the legwork and selected only the top properties for their listings. To ensure that the home is a good fit for you, you also receive a ton of additional information, such as floor plans and an expert review.

BookingsForYou.com: If you are seeking a unique apartment or villa for your trip to Italy, particularly in the lakes, Tuscany, or Puglia regions, Bookings for You is the perfect website to visit. Beautiful lodging, insider information, and personalized attention are the characteristics of every Booking for You encounter.

Airbnb: Although we have utilized Airbnb extensively in Italy, we are discovering that Booking.com and VRBO offer better rates and booking terms.

CHAPTER 3- EXPLORING THE AMALFI COAST

ICONIC ATTRACTIONS

AMALFI CATHEDRAL

A malfi Cathedral is a Roman Catholic building from the ninth century in Amalfi, Italy's Piazza del Duomo. The apostle Saint Andrew is the object of devotion. Its architecture, which is mostly Arab-Norman Romanesque, has undergone multiple remodels that have added Byzantine, Gothic, Baroque, and Romanesque components. The Cathedral includes the adjoining ninth-century Basilica of the Crucifix. Some stairs go to St. Andrew's Crypt from the basilica.

The Amalfi Cathedral's past:

The older basilica, constructed on the remains of an earlier temple, was placed next to the more recent Cathedral. The bones of St. Andrew were delivered to Amalfi from Constantinople in 1206 during the Fourth Crusade by Cardinal Peter of Capua. Upon completion in 1208, the church received the relics. Later, speculation was that Manna would emerge from the saint's bones.

The Amalfi Cathedral's interior:

In the liturgical space is a wooden Crucifix from the thirteenth century. To the right of the rear entrance is another crucifix made of mother-of-pearl. This crucifix was speculated to have been brought from the Holy Land. The sarcophagus of Archbishop Pietro Capuano, who passed away in 1214, served as the foundation for the High Altar in the central nave. Andrea Dell'Asta painted The Martyrdom of St. Andrew over the altar. The artwork on the 1702 boxed ceiling features the Crucifixion of the Apostle, the Flagellation, and the Miracle of the Manna by Dell'Asta from 1710. Two columnar pieces of Egyptian granite support the triumphal arch. Two more twisted columns and two pulpits from the ambo of the twelfth century remain.

The Amalfi Cathedral's exterior:

The Cathedral was rebuilt after the original front facade fell in 1891. The new Cathedral was built with striped marble, stone, open arches, and lace details, uncommon in Italian religious architecture. Still, the tiled cupola is quite typical of the local churches. The mosaics on the tympanum depict "The Triumph of Christ," an artwork by Domenico Morelli, whose original drawings are still in the Town Hall.

Opening Hours:
Daily from March to June 9:00 - 18:45

Daily from July to September 9:00 - 19:45
Daily from November to February 10:00 - 13.00 & 14:30 - 16:30
NOTE: Free admission to the Cathedral during religious functions.

AMALFI CATHEDRAL
Piazza Duomo, 84011 Amalfi SA

+39 089.871324
Amalfi Tourist Office Ticket price: three€

VILLA RUFOLO, RAVELLO

Constructed in the 13th century by a prosperous family of merchants, the villa boasts a long and fascinating history. One can find a narrative about the villa and its owner in Boccaccio's Decameron, one of the first works of Italian Renaissance literature released in 1353.

It was formerly among the most wealthy and big villas on the Amalfi Coast, and rumors of buried money there flourished.

The Rufolo family entertained King Robert II of Naples and other Norman nobility at banquets in the fourteenth century.

Sir Francis Neville Reid:

Numerous rooms in the villa had collapsed due to age and disrepair when Scottish botanist Sir Francis Neville Reid paid a visit in 1851. But Reid was enthralled with the scenery and the Moorish towers. After buying the villa, he extensively renovated the remaining rooms and the gardens.

The city of Music Ravello is still home to Wagner's soul today.

Ravello is presently called "la città della musica," or the city of music. For the past few decades, the Villa Rufolo has been the focal point of an annual summer concert series that includes chamber music, piano concerts, and an enormous orchestra performance on a stage that overlooks the untamed Amalfi Coast below and the Mediterranean Sea.

Gardens at Villa Rufolo:

The Villa Rufolo's grounds and gardens are open year-round and draw tourists from all over the world.

The gardens, with their abundance of flowers, have a magical quality compared to the sea, the sky, umbrella trees, and the Church of the Annunziata below.

PATH OF THE GODS HIKE

Sentiero degli Dei, often known as the Path of the Gods, is a stunning walking route in Italy above the seaside towns of Positano and Praiano. With its breathtaking views of Positano and the Sorrento peninsula, this hike is the most well-liked one on the Amalfi Coast. This guide covers all the specifics of hiking the Path of the Gods.

When to Hike the Path of the Gods:

Because of the Mediterranean environment on the Amalfi Coast, the Path of the Gods is open year-round. There are more people and warmer weather in the summer, which is an excellent excuse to cool off in Positano's pristine waters after your climb. If you decide to trek this route during the summer, start early to avoid hiking during the hottest part of the day because there is extraordinarily little shade.

As with any trek, it is better to leave early! It is a few steps to reach the path without a cab or your vehicle, so it is crucial to board the bus early before it gets crowded and hot.

Getting Up and Down:

Since the Path of the Gods is primarily downhill, hiking it from the village of Bomerano is modest. The trail descends over 500 meters over about 4.7 miles (7.5 kilometers). As previously said, the hike takes two to four hours to finish. You will want plenty of time to take in all the views, so I recommend an additional four hours.

Reaching the Path:

The renowned beach city of Positano is reachable via Nocelle, the little mountain village of Bomerano, and the Path of the Gods. While you can start trekking the Path of the Gods from either end, we advise beginning in Bomerano at Piazza Paolo Capass. One reason is that the hike starts in Bomerano and goes downward, with steep stairs. It also indicates that you will finish in Positano, where you may enjoy a wonderful lunch and a beach day.

Route Map for the Gods' Path:

If you are visiting Italy from overseas and cannot access cellular service, I advise downloading the Amalfi Coast region to your offline Google Maps application.

The public SITA bus, private shuttle, or taxi can all take you to the head of the trail.

A taxi from Positano to Bomerano costs roughly 40 euros, while from Amalfi to Bomerano, it costs 25 euros.

Take the bus to Bomeranos' The Path of the Gods, which is at the head of the trail. Although the hike was relatively easy, public transportation to the trail presented some difficulties. The hub for all the buses is Amalfi Town, where we stayed, which meant that we would need to take a bus to Amalfi Town and then another one from Amalfi to Bomerano to reach the head of the trail.

You must also take two buses unless you stay in Amalfi town or along the Amalfi-Bomerano route.

For trips lasting less than 45 minutes, the SITA bus costs €2.20 one way or €6.80 for a full-day pass. Since most of our trips involved many buses, we were usually better off buying the all-day pass.

Purchasing bus tickets the day before will ensure that you may be on the path first thing in the morning. Many ticket offices and convenience stores that sell tickets open at 8 a.m. or later, and one cannot purchase tickets on the bus.

TIPS FOR HIKING THE TRAIL:

Get some lunch in Bomerano!

Even though we only had a little time in Bomerano, we visited Panificio and enjoyed some of the most excellent pastries we ever had in Italy. We also got some sandwiches to eat on the path before the trip. We quickly stopped at a tiny salumeria where we got some focaccia, salami, and fiordilatte, a cheese from the area that tasted like fresh mozzarella.

Fill water bottles as you go along the path.

There is water available on the path. "Drinkable water" signage will be present. We discovered several water faucets by Just packing a reusable water bottle on the route.

Restrooms

There is a location to get some freshly squeezed lemonade near the finish of the climb, just before you descend the stairs. A small plaza featuring many benches and a public restroom is present. Resting here is a fantastic place to unwind and enjoy the scenery before going into town.

HIDDEN GEMS

FURORE FJORD

Furore Fjord

In the heart of Italy's Amalfi Coast, a fiord boom and a "town that does not exist."

"The town that does not exist" is how many refer to the magnificently named Furore ('Fury' in Italian). Furore, in contrast to many small Italian towns and villages, is made up of a scattering of tiny dwellings perched atop the rock face rather than a big square or town center.

The name of **Furore** comes from Terra Furoris, or 'land of fury,' which dates back to the first settlers along this corner of the coastline who were affected by the roar of the waves that crash into the Fiordo di Furore (Fjord of Furore) during storms. In the past, the town was a small fortress inhabited by a handful of locals under the rule of nearby Amalfi. Thanks to its unique geographic position, the fortress was impenetrable.

How to Reach the Furore Beach and Fjord:

Travelers must travel the Campania coast route, which zigzags through the olive fields and terraced vineyards between Positano and Amalfi, close to Conca dei Marini, to reach Furore. Eventually, the road makes a series of stomach-churning twists and drops precipitously towards the sea, appearing to terminate in the Fjord's deep blue waters. The Fjord resulted from the Schiato torrent, whose bed is now always dry. It is a natural wonder often found in far colder climates.

You must descend the 200 steps of the stairway that starts at the coastal highway above to get to the small beach tucked away at the base of the cliffs. The "Amalfi - Sorrento" route has a Sita bus stop on the bridge above; if you are traveling from Salerno, you will need to change buses in Amalfi.

Furore Fjord beach is shaded in the early afternoon when the sun sets behind the cliffs, so if you want to laze around and enjoy the sun, get there as early as possible. There is a stand where you may rent beach umbrellas and sun loungers, but the beach itself is free and becomes crowded.

Parking in Furore:

Parking at Furore is almost impossible. The only local option is to park in one of the lots for the restaurant La Locanda del Fiordo or Euroconca and have lunch or dinner there, as there is no street parking available for cars or scooters. About two kilometers away, Marina di Praia in Praiano is the closest parking lot to Furore. If not, park your vehicle in Conca de Marini or Amalfi and take the bus to the Fjord.

What to See in Furore:

Several freshly rebuilt "monazzeni" (ancient sheds where fishermen once kept their gear) are visible on the shore at the base of the high cliffs. In the past, these sheds have been home to characters like Ruggieri di Agerola, the fabled bandit mentioned in Boccaccio's Decameron.

Near the "monazzeni" is a historic paper factory that houses Furore's Eco-Museum and botanical garden. It still has a paper press and a mill.

Whether from Capri, other cities on the Campania region's coast, or Naples, a boat excursion is one of the most remarkable ways to observe the beach and Fjord.

Where to Eat In Furore:

The main ingredients of the regional specialties are fresh fish and seafood. Make a reservation at Hostaria Bacco Furore to indulge in traditional delights. Wine enthusiasts may associate the name Furore with the award-winning vintages produced by the Marisa Cuomo winery. You can unwind with a wine tasting while seeing the winery and vineyards that ascend the narrow, steep terraces.

The Furore murals:

Until the 1990s, the only route connecting the high and low regions of the region was the approximately 3000 steps that connect the Fjord with the Furore dwellings. These steps connect with the Sentiero degli Dei and climb to the height of Agerola.

Furore is a part of the Associazione Paesi Dipinti Italiani, an association of painted towns in Italy, and well-known worldwide artists created the murals on the walls of its homes.

See the recently found cycle of frescoes by the Giotto school in the 11th-century Church of San Giacomo Apostolo, a visitor must-see.

Visit the Chiesa di San Michele, which has an asymmetrical entrance, and the Chiesa di Sant'Elia, whose intriguing stratification draws geologists to it frequently. Like the entire Amalfi Coast, Furore is a UNESCO-listed World Heritage Site.

ATRANI

Atrani

Amalfi's twin resembles an enchanted Italian nativity scene with its labyrinth of tiny lanes, slender staircases, and homes perched on the rocks just above the Mediterranean.

A fishing village whose history is similar to that of its famous neighbor, Amalfi, and which has managed to preserve its old medieval architecture, which consists of a series of buildings dotted with narrow alleyways, covered tunnels, and tiny gardens, all remarkably intact. The remotest village in Southern Italy, Atrani, is perched on a cliff face at the mouth of the Valle del Dragone, just above the sea.

How to Get to Atrani:

The modest village of Atrani is adjacent to the bustling center of Amalfi, about a kilometer further along the coast of Campania. The A3 Napoli-Salerno route connects Vietri sul Mare and Atrani. Follow the SS163, a well-known coastal route that stretches the entire length of the Amalfi Coast, from Vietri for roughly 20 kilometers to Atrani. Capodichino Airport in Naples is the closest airport. Alternatively, the SITA bus from Salerno or Sorrento that travels to Amalfi might take you to Atrani.

What to See in Atrani:

The renowned Amalfitana coast road now separates the town and the sea, so anyone wanting to go to the seaside must use one of the passageways like Piazza Umberto I, which was built initially as a boat shelter during high tide and now looks like the backstage area of a theater facing the sea. The **Church of San Salvatore de' Birecto** is the site of the former coronation of the Doges of the Republic of Amalfi.

The glittering majolica-domed **Collegiate Church of Santa Maria Maddalena**, which commands the entire eastern side of the town with its baroque-style facade and tall bell tower, is another site worth seeing, if only for its breathtakingly panoramic perspective.

The Grotta di Masaniello is located next to the church. The local folklore holds that the revolutionists took sanctuary in this cave close to his mother's house. The 11th-century Church of Santa Maria del Bando, perched against the rocks below the Torre dello Zito, is charming and offers a fantastic perspective over Atrani.

Traditional festivals in Atrani:

Santa Maddalena (Mary Magdalene), patron saint of Atrani (22 July)

Reenactment of the Ducal wedding (April)

Sagra del pesce azzurro (August)

What to Eat in Atrani:

Fresh fish dominate Atrani's cuisine. At the same time, there are some non-fish dishes as well, such as sarchiapone, a marrow filled with cheese and meat and cooked in tomato sauce, custard- and-cherry-filled pasticciotto, and the delectably sweet cassata atranese. Ristorante Savò serves visually stunning and delectable gourmet cuisine in the tiny town square. A family of former fishermen owns Paranza and serves simpler meals.

Sarchiapone

Other tasty treats:
   Scialatielli alle vongole veraci

Colatura di Alici

Involtini di mozzarella in foglia di limone

Delizia al limoncello

Involtini di mozzarella in foglia di limone

CHAPTER 4: SAVORING THE FLAVORS

CULINARY DELIGHTS

LOCAL DISHES TO TRY

Y ou must have several delicacies while visiting the Amalfi Coast, as anyone with a sweet appetite will attest to. Contrary to widespread belief, this area contains authentic and delicious foods with many more food pairings than only citrus flavors.

Treat yourself to a gourmet journey, discovering them all. Savor every recipe, from starters to sweets, and immerse yourself in the multi-sensory sensation of aroma, taste, and sight. I promise you will always hold these "new" flavors close to your heart.

Here are the top 5 dishes you must try while visiting the Amalfi Coast and recommendations for where to eat them!

Ricotta and mozzarella cheese:

Agerola, a tiny settlement in the Lattari Mountains that resembles a balcony with a view of the Amalfi Coast, is an excellent place to start. Take a break and treat yourself to a tasting at one of the many picturesque farmhouses in the area. The provola affummicata, or smoked provola, is incredibly delicious. Still, it would be best to try the Fior di latte. This mozzarella serves as the base for the Caprese salad, which also features local tomatoes and cheeses, the most delicious of which is the Provolone del Monaco. Every flavor is genuine and unmatched anywhere.

Cetar Anchovies:

You must sample the anchovies in Cetara, whether fried, marinated, or fried in oil. Either way, they're too good to resist and make a great appetizer! The anchovies are salted and pressed after being fished, which generally happens in the spring. The fish prepared this way releases a liquid called colatura, which is bottled and used as a seasoning once exposed to the sun. Please do not pass up a dish of linguine or spaghetti with this sauce; it has a flavor that the Japanese refer to as umami, which is robust but well-balanced. Rest assured, you will not regret it!

Cetar Anchovies

The Amalfitana Scialatielli:

The irregularly shaped Scialatielli is a staple of the Amalfi Coast's fresh pasta cuisine. I suggest you try it in Amalfi, where Chef Cosentino created them. They have fewer eggs in the dough and use flour and water instead of other fresh pasta varieties.

The Scialatielli pairs incredibly well with seafood, though they also pair nicely with many other sauces. This dish will tempt you to have another helping!

Pizza Tramonti's:

When one thinks about Campania cuisine, pizza immediately comes to mind. Only some people know Tramonti, on the Amalfi Coast, is where the original version originated. Wholemeal flour combined with fennel and a selection of items is incorporated to make the topping, including Corbarino tomato, Colline Salernitana DOP oil, and the delectable Fior di Latte mozzarella from Monti Lattari.

Nothing more needs to be said; try it and allow the deliciousness to entice you!

Pasta stuffed with lemon:

The authentic essence of the Amalfi Coast may be experienced in Positano when you order a plate of pasta, known as tagliolini, with lemon and enjoy it while taking in the stunning sea view. Fresh pasta and lemons are two typical ingredients that refresh tagliolini with lemon. With its sour touch, the citrus sauce used for the dressing creates a distinctive flavor that evokes summer and holidays. It is so simple and delicious that it astounds. Easy and flawless.

BEST RESTAURANTS AND CAFES

Kasai · Praiano:

The beautiful village of Praiano is between Positano and Amalfi Town. In this more relaxed and laid-back neighborhood, one can find some of the most excellent eateries on the Amalfi Coast. One of those eateries is called Kasai, which offers seafood selections along with some fantastic meat entrees like lamb or beef. And some delicious sweets as well. The balcony provides unparalleled views of the Tyrrhenian Sea. But also note how tastefully and hospitably designed the interior dining area is.

Address: Via Umberto I, 84, 84010 Praiano SA, Italy
   Must-try dish: Roast lamb & lemon cake for dessert. Visit the Website
   Ristorante Franchino · Praiano:

Praiano's location allows many eateries with breathtaking views of the surrounding area and the open sea. The east side of town's Ristorante Franchino is the same. It is the perfect spot to enjoy homemade pasta and fresh seafood dishes while taking in the sunset. Situated in the same family-run, four-star Onda Verde Hotel for almost forty years, this establishment offers top-notch cuisine, impeccable service, and a prime location.

Address: Via Terramare, 3, 84010 Praiano SA, Italy
   Must try dish: Catch of the day Visit Website

Il Pirata Restaurant · Praiano:

Il Pirata Ristorante, Lounge Bar & Beach Club is closer to the water, immediately beneath Ristorante Franchino. It is a superb spot to spend the day on a sunbed, enjoy a few cocktails at the open bar while seeing the boats enter and exit the harbor, or have dinner in their excellent restaurant. All the while, enjoy the very stunning vistas. Seafood is the main course once more. There are many beautiful dishes, such as monkfish with crispy potatoes or blue lobster linguine.

On the other hand, they also serve some excellent steak sliced with lettuce, tomatoes, and cheese. A great atmosphere is created by the lighting at night and the proximity to the ocean—an absolute must-see in Praiano.

A Popular Monkfish Dish

DINING AND WINING RECOMMENDATIONS

Lemon-infused Dishes with Falanghina:

Dish Ideas: Consider trying "Linguine al Limone" (Lemon Linguine) or "Calamari al Limone" (Lemon-infused Calamari).

Wine Pairing: Falanghina, with its bright acidity and citrus notes, enhances the zesty flavors of lemon-infused dishes, creating a refreshing and harmonious pairing.

Seafood Pasta with Fiano di Avellino:

Dish Ideas: Opt for a classic "Spaghetti alle Vongole" (Clam Pasta) or "Linguine ai Frutti di Mare" (Mixed Seafood Linguine).

Wine Pairing: Fiano di Avellino's floral and fruity characteristics complement the saltiness of seafood, offering a well-balanced combination that captures the essence of the Amalfi Coast.

Mozzarella and Tomato Caprese with Greco di Tufo:

Dish Ideas: Enjoy a traditional Caprese salad with locally sourced mozzarella, ripe tomatoes, and fresh basil.

Wine Pairing: Greco di Tufo's crisp acidity and mineral undertones provide a delightful contrast to mozzarella's creaminess while enhancing the tomatoes' vibrant flavors.

Grilled Fish with Aglianico:

Dish Ideas: Choose a locally caught fish, such as branzino or sea bass, prepare it with olive oil, herbs, and a touch of lemon, then grill or bake.

Wine Pairing: Aglianico's bold tannin and dark fruit flavors complement the robust taste of grilled fish, creating a savory and satisfying pairing.

Pizza Margherita with Rosato (Rosé) Wine:

Dish Ideas: Savor the simplicity of a classic Margherita pizza with tomato, mozzarella, and basil.

Wine Pairing: A light and crisp Rosato (Rosé) wine adds a refreshing element to the pizza, balancing the acidity of the tomato and the creaminess of the mozzarella.

VISITING WINERIES

WINE TASTING EXPERIENCES

A lovely experience, wine tasting on the Amalfi Coast allows you to visit nearby vineyards, sample unique wines, and take in the breathtaking views. The following wine-tasting events are prevalent along the Amalfi Coast:

Winery Marisa Cuomo (Furore):

Highlights: Views of the sea from a clifftop vineyard.

Wines: "Ravello Rosso" red wine and "Fiorduva" white blend.

Montani's Tenuta San Francesco:

Highlights: Traditional winemaking in Tramonti.

Wines: "Biancolella" white, "Costa d'Amalfi" red.

"Costa d'Amalfi" Red

San Cipriano Picentino's Montevetrano Winery:

Highlights: The "Montevetrano" red mix is almost flawless.

In Raito, Vietri sul Mare is Le Vigne di Raito:

Highlights: Charming boutique winery near Vietri sul Mare.

Wines: "Rosamara" rosé, produced in small quantities.

Marisa Cuomo, cantine (Tramonti):

The highlights of Azienda Agricola San Francesco (Furore) are the modern-traditional synthesis of "Furore Bianco Fiorduva."

Highlights: Furore's organic winery is family-owned and operated.

Wines: red "Per Eva" and white "PietraCupa"

TOURING VINEYARDS WITH BREATHTAKING VIEWS

CASA SETARO

Devotion to Winemaking

The estate and winery of Casa Setaro are on the foothills of the renowned Mount Vesuvius in the Italian wine region of Campania. The Setaro family's love and passion were the foundation of the winery. The family grows grapes, produces sustainable wines, and resurrects endangered vine species.

Location:

Via Cifelli 10, 80040 Trecase Naples, Italy

VISITING HOURS:

MONDAY: 09:30 - 18:30 TUESDAY: 09:30 - 18:30 WEDNESDAY: 09:30 - 18:30 THURSDAY: 09:30 - 18:30 FRIDAY: 09:30 - 18:30 SATURDAY: 09:30 - 18:30 SUNDAY: 09:30 - 18:30

WINE TYPES:
RED WINE
WHITE WINE
ROSE WINE
ORANGE WINE
SPARKLING WINE
SWEET WINE
FORTIFIED WINE
SPIRITS

Grape Varieties:
Caprettone, Piedirosso, Falanghina, Aglianico

Our Experiences:

Discover the passion and affection of the Casa Setaro family estate for €70.00.

Everyone can enjoy a variety of wine-tasting experiences provided by Casa Setaro. One can further tailor the various experiences to their interests. Visits to the vineyard and cellar include the price of every wine-tasting expertise in the estate house sandwiched between the sea and the volcano. The 'degustazione con 5 vini' wine tasting consists of a sample of five exceptional Casa Setaro estate wines and a walk in the vineyard with views of the Vesuvius National Park.

Experience Highlights
  Winery: Casa Setaro
  Activity type: Visit & Tasting
  Experience duration:0 Hour 30 Minutes
  Things to see: Vineyards, Winery, Tasting Room

MASTROBERARDINO

Mastroberardino is a historic family estate with three centuries of winemaking history. The narrative begins in the village of Atripalda, in the heart of the Irpinia wine area, when Berardino, who received the title "Maestro," established his first winery in the seventeenth century. The present owner, Professor Piero Mastroberardino, Cavalier Angelo's great-great-grandfather, legally registered the farm in 1878.

The restoration project of the historic vineyards at Villa dei Misteri:

Villa dei Misteri was the name given to the restoration effort of the historic vines. The primary goal is to reconstruct this region's vineyards, grape varieties, farming methods, and wine manufacturing processes before Mount Vesuvius's explosion during the Roman era. 2001 saw the introduction of the first vintages from old vineyards. This time-traveling machine can transfer to the past in the era of Ancient Rome; it is a miracle to try what was previously served in the taverns of Pompeii to comprehend and experience life as they lived many years ago.

Location
Via Manfredi 75-81, Atripalda, Avellino, 83042, Italy

Visiting Hours:
Monday: 09:30 - 16:00
Tuesday: 09:30 - 16:00 Wednesday: 09:30 - 16:00
Thursday: 09:30 - 16:00 Friday: 09:30 - 16:00
Saturday: closed. Sunday: closed.

Grape varieties:
Aglianico, Fiano, Greco, Falanghina, Coda Di Volpe

Wine types:
Red Wine
White Wine
Rose Wine
Orange Wine
Sparkling Wine
Sweet Wine
Fortified Wine
Spirits

Our Experiences:

WINE TASTING AND TOUR AT MASTROBERARDINO

At Mastroberardino, sample traditional wines from native Campania vines, tour the vineyards, and discover the winemaking process. Do you want to see the attractions of Campania and add some excitement to your life with an exciting wine tourism adventure? If so, be ready to enjoy the delights of wine tasting by packing your bags and taking a flight to Mastroberardino, one of the most renowned wineries in Italy.

When you arrive at the estate, a tour of the vineyards will reveal the resurgence of native grape varietals, and you can observe the meticulous production and aging process in the winery and cellar. Finish by sampling a wide choice of red, white, and dessert wines.

Experience Highlights Winery: Mastroberardino
    Activity type: Visit & Tasting
    Experience duration: 1 Hour 30 Minutes
    Tasted wines: 1 - 3.
    Wine types: Red Wine, White Wine, Sweet Wine
    Things to see: Vineyards, Winery, Cellar

Location
    Via Manfredi 75-81, Atripalda, Avellino, 83042, Italy
    €20

CANTINA DEL VESUVIO WINERY

Uncover the Volcano's Wine

Located on the picturesque slopes of Mount Vesuvius, the Cantina del Vesuvio Winery started in 1948. The Cantina del Vesuvio is between

Pompeii and the crater on the slopes of Vesuvius. The Gulf of Naples, the Sorrento Peninsula, and Capri Island surround the Campania region. It benefits from a great environment and fertile terrain that produces delicious grapes. The estate spans over sixteen hectares and is within the Vesuvius National Park. The current owner, Maurizio Russo, has continued the family tradition of crafting a small batch of the best wines, each year featuring a different variety.

Location
Via Panoramica 65, Trecase, 80040, Italy

Sub-region:
Vesuvio, Campania

Visiting Hours:
Monday: 11:00 - 16:00
Tuesday: 11:00 - 16:00 Wednesday: 11:00 - 16:00 Thursday: 11:00 - 16:00 Friday: 11:00 - 16:00
Saturday: 11:00 - 16:00 Sunday: 11:00 - 16:00

Wine types:
Red Wine
White Wine
Rose Wine
Sparkling Wine
Sweet Wine
Fortified Wine

Grape varieties:
Caprettone, Piedirosso

Our Experiences:

WINE TASTING AND TOUR AT CANTINA DEL VESUVIO WINERY:

A trip here is an adventure as well as a source of enjoyment. Take a guided walk tour of Vesuvius with a member of the Russo Family. The journey starts with a stroll through the vineyards, where you can take in breathtaking views of the Gulf of Naples, Sorrento, and the island of Capri. Eventually, you will visit the winery that produces Lacryma Christi DOC and sit down on the patio for a wine tasting, along with typical local delights from this small pocket of paradise on Mount Vesuvius.

Experience Highlights
  Winery: Cantina Del Vesuvio Winery
  Activity type: Visit & Tasting
  Experience duration: 2 Hours and 0 Minutes
  Things to see: Vineyards, Winery, Cellar, Tasting Room, Laboratory, and Other Estate Areas

Cantina Del Vesuvio Winery

AZIENDA AGRICOLA II CONVENTO

How The Winery Originated

The sole male heir, Peppe Pollio, took over the family farm, Il Convento, when he was just 15 years old, having already helped his father out in the countryside after graduating high school. He started his tremendous interest in agriculture and the natural world as a direct farmer. He decided to diversify the company's system in the 1990s, starting with bottling wine and then moving on to oil, which increased overall production. He decided to turn lemons into limoncello in 1995, and it was an instant hit.

Location
   Via Bagnulo 10, 80061 Massa Lubrense Naples, Italy

Visiting Hours:
   Monday: 09:00 - 13:00
   Tuesday: 09:00 - 13:00 Wednesday: 09:00 - 13:00 Thursday: 09:00 - 13:00 Friday: 09:00 - 13:00
   Saturday: 09:00 - 13:00 Sunday: 09:00 - 13:00

Wine types:
   Spirits

Grape varieties:
   Limone di Sorrento IGP

Our Experiences:

LIMONCELLO TOUR AND TASTING AT AZIENDA AGRICOLA IL CONVENTO

A Fascinating Sample €20.00

The Convent invites you to enjoy a genuine limoncello experience inside their luxurious lemon orchards. The Il Convento winery, which makes a variety of liqueurs, including its signature product, limoncello, is where your trip will start. Discover the process of making their limoncello here, as it has a legacy through the years. After that, you will go to Il Convento's lemon groves, where you may learn about the different farming methods on the Sorrento peninsula.

At last, you will arrive at the Il Convento farmhouse, where you can partake in a tasting of their extra virgin olive oil and homemade citrus jams, as well as a variety of their liqueurs, including Limoncello, Arancello, Mandarinetto, Crema di Limoni, Licorice, and the Nocillo. During the tasting, someone will inform you of the history of the building and the company.

Experience Highlights Winery: Agricola Il Convento
   Activity type: Visit & Tasting
   Experience duration: 1 Hour 15 Minutes
   Tasted wines: 4.
   Wine types: Spirits
   Things to see: Cellar, Tasting Room, Laboratory, and Other Estate Areas

Limoncello

CHAPTER 5: EXHILARATING ACTIVITIES

WATER ADVENTURES

BOAT TOURS ALONG THE COAST

The Capri Boat:

T his tour will take you to the port of Marina Grande in around thirty minutes, where you may see the island, have a coffee, and go shopping.

The tour's second destination will undoubtedly be an island excursion. You can stop the boat at any moment to dip in the Capri Sea's pristine waters, including the Green Cave, White Cave, Faraglioni, and Blue Cave.

Capri Sea and Tour Boat

The trip package includes the following services: beach towels, snorkeling gear, prosecco-infused aperitif, soft drinks, snacks, and fuel.

Duration: 8 hours
   Embark port: Castellammare di Stabia - Seiano - Sorrento - Massa Lubrense

Includes:
   Snack & Drink
   Transportation

Boat Tour Amalfi and Positano Services:

We will pause to take in an authentic little paradise when we reach the Island of li Galli, which should take around thirty minutes. The second destination is the fishing village and historic city of Amalfi, where we will tour the Paper Museum and the Cathedral.

The picturesque Positano, where guests can descend to take in the village's splendor, will be the third destination. While traveling between Amalfi and Positano, we will stop in the picturesque village of Praiano and the Furore Fjord, regarded as one of Italy's most scenic locations. On the way back, we will also see the stunning island of Eduardo de Filippo and the Crapolla fjord.

The tour package includes the following services: transportation to and from the hotel, complimentary parking, petrol, a prosecco-infused aperitif, soft drinks, snacks, beach towels, and snorkeling gear.

Private boat tour of Ischia Island:

Ischia, the most oversized island in the Gulf of Naples, is well-known for its thermal waters, stunning scenery, and famous spas. Thousands of travelers from all over the world visit the island each year. In addition, there are numerous creeks to explore and the renowned Aragonese castle on the island of Ischia.

Ischia boat trip description: We will arrive at the solitary island of Ischia in about fifty minutes, at which point we will tour the island to take in all its many splendors.

The most stunning locations on the island, including **San Angelo, San Montano, San Pancrazio,** and the well-known **Green Cave**, will no longer be hidden from you.

Grotto Verde (Green Cave)

Savor the view of the breathtaking scenery and the abundance of nature all around you. We will visit various features of Ischia during the day, including crowded beaches, hidden creeks, caverns, and inlets.

The trip package includes the following services: beach towels, snorkeling gear, prosecco-infused aperitif, soft drinks, snacks, and fuel.

SNORKELING AND DIVING SPOTS

Snorkeling with Marine Biologist Expert from Sorrento:

Summary:

Get more out of your time in the sea at Sorrento with a snorkel session led by a marine biologist guide. You will visit a marine life-rich protected section of the coastline close to Punta Campanella in a small group of no more than ten individuals. Discover the untamed coastline surrounding Sorrento before diving in with a marine biology specialist to snorkel among bream, barracudas, and, with any luck, dolphins and sea turtles.

Use the wet suit, mask, and snorkel provided to make the experience lighter.

Discover more from a specialist about the Sorrentine Peninsula's aquatic life.

Investigate the waters surrounding Punta Campanella's coastal nature reserve.

What's Included:

Use of Snorkeling equipment
    All Fees and Taxes
    Snacks

Meeting point
    Via Marina Grande, 186
    Via Marina Grande, 186, 80067 Sorrento NA, Italy
    Punta Campanella Diving Sorrento

Endpoint
    This activity ends back at the meeting point.

What To Anticipate

You will encounter limestone cliffs, caverns, and gullies teeming with sponges and madrepores. Admire the protected marine area's splendor in the company of our marine biologist. The fortunate ones may also see dolphins and turtles at specific times of the year. Hedgehogs, starfish, and seahorses are frequently spotted, though.

Kayaking & Snorkeling in Amalfi Coast, Maiori, Sea caves, and beach:

Summary

You can be sure of an authentic, safe, and one-of-a-kind experience from the local guides and instructors with years of experience in the field. The bespoke adjustable kayak seats ensure optimal comfort throughout the journey, making them unsinkable and self-emptying.

In addition, the kayak courses are well-instructed, so even inexperienced kayakers can enjoy them.

We are holding out for you!

All necessary kayak equipment and safety gear are included for an utterly secure adventure.

Take pictures to capture your kayaking experience forever—skilled native tour guides for a distinctive and genuine encounter.

What's Included

Kayaks, paddles, life jackets, dry bags, snorkeling equipment, hats
HQ photo shoot (Someone will send you photos by email after the
tour is over)
Snacks

Meeting point Cooperative Boating Maiori Via Giovanni Amendola,
84010 Maiori SA, Italy

Start time 10:00 a.m.

Endpoint This activity ends back at the meeting point.

What To Expect

We will prepare to set sail westward towards "Amalfi" following a quick
explanation of the itinerary and a brief introduction course on navigating and maritime safety. We can watch the "Monti Lattari" dive into the
water as we cruise down the shore, creating an unpredictable spectacle!
This part will take you through the coast's historic settlements. We will
be able to see sea caves of all kinds and forms, freshwater waterfalls
like Marmorata's that empty straight into the ocean, and undiscovered
beaches that are only reachable by boat. Several private villas that scale
the rocks will be visible.

KAYAKING IN HIDDEN COVES

Amalfi - Runghetiello Grotto (Half Day Tour):

Duration: 3 hours
Distance: 9 Km 5.6 Miles
Experience: Beginner, Intermediate

DEPARTURE / RETURN LOCATION: Lido Delle Sirene Beach
Inclusions:
English-speaking local guides and instructors
Photos will be sent by email once the tour has ended.
Bottled water.
Snacks
fresh fruit
Facilities
changing rooms, restrooms, and luggage storage

Introductory lesson
kayaks, paddles, life jackets, waterproof jackets, watertight bags,
snorkeling equipment, and hats

Route: Upon donning our life jackets and adjusting the footrests on
our kayaks, we will prepare to depart westward in the direction of the
Runghetiello Grotto.

There will be a brief introduction to kayaking and marine safety for
individuals who have never used a kayak.

Our path will take us past some of the best beaches in Amalfi, past
naturally occurring rock arches, and into sea caves where we can get
a close-up look at the historic watch towers scattered throughout the
coast.

We will stop at beaches that can only be accessed by boat, giving us time
to swim or snorkel in the pristine seas.

Not too far from the starting point, after passing the beaches of Duoglio
and Santa Croce, we will kayak by the "Arc of Lovers," a naturally
occurring rock arch whose shape resembles two elephants sharing a
kiss and was formed millions of years ago by sea erosion. Young couples
used to get married on top of it not too long ago.

Later, we will paddle by Sophia Loren's villa and pass the old "Il
Saraceno" hotel on La Vite Beach before passing in front of the historic
fisherman's village of Conca dei Marini.

We will also have a breathtaking view of the Santa Rosa Monastery,
formerly a Dominican nuns' residence and now a luxurious hotel.

The delectable "Sfogliatella Santa Rosa," a shell-shaped pastry filled with a cream made with ricotta cheese and tiny pieces of dried fruit, which is a staple of the region's culinary culture, originated right in these monastic kitchens (be sure to sample it before you go!).

After passing Conca dei Marini's seaside, we will approach its western basin, from where we will have a stunning view of the settlements of Furore and Praiano, as well as the islands of Li Galli and Capri and the well-known Faraglioni Rocks.

Finally, we will locate and explore the small Runghetiello Grotto, a charming natural sea cave named for a local fish, featuring vivid red and green mineral frescoes on its walls. It is farther into this basin.

We shall see the sea and country in a new, but no less spectacular, way back to Amalfi.

Essential information

Double kayaks, which are incredibly stable and easy to maneuver, will be provided for each participant. If a party has an odd number of people, just one kayak will be available.

Amalfi - Maiori:

Duration: ~3 hours **Distance:** 10 Km 6.2 Miles
Experience: Beginner Intermediate

DEPARTURE / RETURN LOCATION:

Lido Delle Sirene Beach

Inclusions:

English-speaking local guides and instructor's Introductory lesson
All the necessary equipment (*check equipment page for more info*)
kayaks, paddles, life jackets, waterproof jackets, watertight bags,
snorkeling equipment, and hats
HQ photo service
: someone will email the photos once the tour ends. Bottled water.
Snacks frutta fresca
Facilities
include changing rooms, restrooms, and luggage storage

Route: After putting on our life jackets and adjusting the footrests on
our kayaks, we will prepare to head east toward Maiori.

There will be a brief introduction to kayaking and marine safety for
individuals who have never used a kayak.

We will see the best beaches in Amalfi, nearby sulfurous springs and
sea caves. Throughout the way, we will see the historic watch towers
scattered throughout the coast.

We will next stop at beaches that can only be accessed by boat, giving
us time to swim or snorkel in the pristine seas.

We will kayak in front of the Saint Andrew Grotto, a sizable natural sea
cave teeming with stalactites named for Amalfi's patron saint, Andrea,

not too far from the starting point, just before reaching the town center.

Then, we will head to the settlements of Atrani and Marmorata, where we will witness some sulfurous spring-filled coves and a mesmerizing waterfall that cascades down the cliffs directly into the sea.

As we paddle farther down the coast, we will see the abundant lemon gardens of Maiori, Minori, and Ravello and stunning houses perched on the edge of sheer cliffs.

What to bring
Recommended items.
Sunscreen (highly recommended)
Change of dry clothes
Towel Recommended attire.
Bathing suit
Light-colored T-shirt (for protection against the sun and preferably made of Lycra)
Wear shoes suitable for water, such as water shoes for kayaking or rubber shoes.
Flip-flops work fine as well.
Hat
Sunglasses with safety cord
Sailing or mountain-biking gloves (if protection for hands is needed)

Essential information

Double kayaks, which are incredibly stable and easy to maneuver, will be provided for each participant. If a party has an odd number of people, just one kayak will be available.

Every tour is a group tour. Contact us to arrange a private trip.

Every client must present an identity document on the day of the tour.

Capri Island (full-day tour):

Duration: ~8 hours
Distance: 15 Km 9.3 Miles
Experience: Advanced

DEPARTURE / RETURN LOCATION

Amalfi (to be agreed)

Inclusions:
English-speaking local guides and instructors
Introductory lesson
All the necessary equipment (check equipment page for more info)
Kayaks, paddles, life jackets, waterproof jackets, watertight bags, snorkeling equipment, hats, and drying towels
HQ photo service: someone will email photos once the tour ends.
Bottled water.
Snacks-fresh fruit, biscuits
Picnic lunch with typical products of Amalfi Coast and Campania
Facilities
Changing rooms, restrooms, and luggage storage
Boat transfer to/from Capri Island

Route

Our private boat will transport us and the kayaks to the gorgeous island of Capri from Amalfi, where the Capri Island trip starts.

We will get a fantastic view of the Amalfi Coast, Li Galli Island, and the Sorrento Peninsula from the water during the 45-minute boat ride.

As soon as we reach the island, we will put our life jackets and kayaks into the water to prepare for the tour.

The most spectacular of all Roman Emperor Tiberius' Island homes, Villa Jovis, will be the first sight just past the starting point.

Next will be the Rock Window to The Sky, a sizable mountain opening formed over millions of years by a unique wind current.

We will soon arrive at the well-known Faraglioni Rocks, three rocky columns that have earned the nickname "guardians of Capri" due to their formation throughout time because of coastal morphological processes.

From here, we can enter a rock tunnel carved out of one of these rocks and go through it.

Next, we will arrive at Marina Piccola Bay, one of the island's two primary beaches, where you may dock and explore on foot.

Following our break, we will explore a network of interconnecting sea caves that the kayak can only reach, such as the Green Grotto (Grotta Verde), where snorkeling is ideal due to the pristine water.

Capri Dock

After that, we will circle the island to locate the Punta Carena Lighthouse and paddle up to the island's most well-known landmark, the Blue Grotto (Grotta Azzurra).

This cavern is roughly 150 meters deep and stretches about 50 meters into the cliff near the surface. The cavern's well-known blue reflection is caused by sunlight entering an underwater chamber. We can access the grotto by swimming or by unique boats (additional charge) depending on when we arrive.

We will explore the Blue Grotto and then return to Amalfi via boat, which ends our journey with a breathtaking vista of one of the most beautiful islands in the world as the sun sets.

What to bring

Recommended items:

Sunscreen (highly recommended)

Change of dry clothes

Towel

Recommended attire:

Bathing suit

Light-colored T-shirt (for protection against the sun and preferably made of Lycra)

Shoes suitable for water, such as water shoes for kayaking or rubber shoes

Flip-flops work fine as well.

Hat

Sunglasses with safety cord

Sailing or mountain-biking gloves (if protection for hands is needed)

Important notes:

All the participants will have double kayaks, which are very stable and easy to manage. In the case of groups with an odd number of participants, the company will provide a single kayak to additional individuals.

All tours are group tours. For private tours, please get in touch with the company.

On the tour day, all clients must show an identity document.

CULTURAL EXPERIENCES

Cultural Italy

LOCAL FESTIVALS AND EVENTS

Along the Amalfi Coast, celebrations and religious events occur all year. Symphony and choir concerts are everywhere during Christmas, and the mood is joyous. Amalfitani people enjoy commemorating holidays.

Along with other celebrations around the coast, Amalfi's main beach welcomes Capodanno, or New Year's, with a massive celebration and spectacular fireworks. There are several reasons to throw extravagant family gatherings with special meals and religious rites, such as the Good Friday candlelight procession, Easter Sunday, and Christmas pageants with crib competitions (with cribs set in the city fountains).

Festa dell'Assunta:

August 15 is Positano's most enormous religious feast and star event of the year when a reenactment of Santa Maria Assunta's Byzantine icon of the Madonna and Child is transported from the church to the sea and celebrated with evening fireworks and music on the main beach. Positano, Campania.

Festa di San' Andrea:

This festival, which takes place on June 27 and November 30, is a religious event dedicated to Amalfi's patron saint and defender of mariners. The summer festival honors the miraculous defeat of a pirate invasion in 1544, while the November festival honors the passing of St. Andrew. A giant silver-gilt statue of the saint was carried by a procession of men wearing white robes through the town, the port, and the shore. The big finish is the statue running—in one spectacular dash—straight up the 62 stairs to the Cathedral. Concerts in Piazza

Duomo and breathtaking fireworks show over the water around the evening in Campania's Amalfi.

Positano Premia La Danza Léonide Massine:

This celebration of dance takes place in the first week of September and includes panel discussions, dance performances, music concerts, gallery exhibits, and an awards ceremony.

Festival of Ravello:

Concerts in the Villa Rufolo's magnificent gardens helped establish Ravello's reputation as the "City of Music," beginning in the 1950s. From June to October, the renowned Ravello Festival offers a wide range of events, including chamber music performances by small ensembles and full orchestras playing works by Wagner, Bach, Mozart, Beethoven, Brahms, Chopin, and lesser-known Italian composers like Scarlatti and Cimarosa. The festival also has excellent jazz, opera, and dance performances, and global pop talents perform live. The most well-known event is the Concerto all'Alba, which takes place on August 10 to coincide with the shooting stars on the night of San Lorenzo. Devoted music enthusiasts wake up at 4:30 to see the sunrise over the bay to the accompaniment of music from a full symphony orchestra. Campania, Ravello, 84010.

The Fish Festival:

This fantastic fish festival takes place on the beach in Fornillo on the last Saturday of September. There's live music and abundant fish and seafood delicacies to sample.

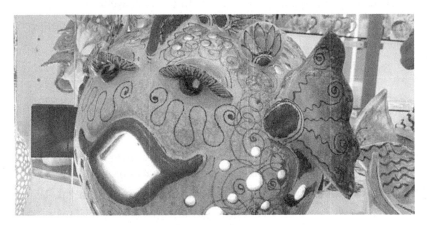

Fish Festival Artwork

TRADITIONAL ART AND CRAFTSMANSHIP

Ceramics:

Description: The Amalfi Coast is famous for its vibrant, hand-painted ceramics. Local artisans craft various items, including tiles, plates, bowls, and decorative pieces.

Techniques: Traditional Majolica techniques involve intricate hand-painting and glazing. Patterns often feature marine motifs, lemons, and scenes inspired by local landscapes.

Paper Art - Amalfi Paper:

Description: Amalfi is renowned for its historic paper mills, producing high-quality handmade paper. This tradition dates back to the Middle Ages.

Techniques: Artisans use traditional methods to create cotton and cellulose pulp paper. The paper is for stationery, journals, and artistic prints.

Wood Inlay (Intarsia):

Description: Local craftsmen on the Amalfi Coast are skilled in wood inlay, known as "intarsia." This technique involves creating intricate designs by embedding diverse types of wood into a base.

Products: Wooden boxes, furniture, and decorative items featuring detailed scenes and patterns.

Limoncello Craftsmanship:

Description: Limoncello, a famous lemon liqueur from the region, is often produced in small, family-owned distilleries. The craftsmanship lies in selecting and peeling the finest local lemons.

Process: The traditional process involves soaking lemon peels in alcohol, creating a flavorful and aromatic liqueur.

Coral Jewelry:

Description: The Amalfi Coast has a long tradition of crafting coral jewelry. Artisans use coral from the Mediterranean Sea to create unique and elegant pieces.

Designs: Coral is often paired with gold or silver to create intricate jewelry designs, including necklaces, earrings, and bracelets.

COOKING CLASSES AND LOCAL MARKET VISITS

Amalfi Coast: Small group Market tour & Cooking Class in Praiano:

Details: Connect with fellow travelers who share your enthusiasm for Italian cuisine.

Visit the bustling local market first, where your host will show you the ins and outs of choosing the best ingredients according to the seasons.

After that, return home for an actual, hands-on cooking session. Enjoy an Italian Aperitivo to warm up and learn how to prepare two regional specialties.

Enjoy the food you have made with regional wines after the class, and toast to your new acquaintances over a glass!

What to Anticipate

Enjoy a hands-on cooking session, immerse yourself in the bustling local market, and share your enthusiasm for Italian cuisine with other charming visitors.

You will visit the local market with your Cesarina host, who will teach you how to select the best ingredients for the season. Then, you will return to their home, warm up with an Italian Aperitivo, and enjoy the class. You will learn how to make two iconic dishes of the city you are visiting.

After the workshop, you will savor everything you make for lunch or dinner with regional wines. Dining this way is ideal if you want to experience authentic connections, cuisine, and friendship while learning about authentic regional Italian gastronomy.

The oldest network of home cooks in Italy, Cesarine, is in more than 500 locations nationwide.

Inclusions

Tasting session (lunch)

Learn to make two iconic recipes.

Share your passion for Italian cuisine with other lovely guests!

Local wines, water, and soft drinks for kids Small Group Market Tour

Italian Market

Sorrento Pizza Making:

Duration: 2 hours (approx.)

Pickup offered.

Mobile ticket

Overview:

Immerse yourself in the art of Italian pizza-making during this cooking class in Sorrento. Learn from your chef/guides, pros at rolling and tossing dough, and picking out the freshest ingredients.

Have fun learning the techniques, tasting olive oil and limoncello, and finally, sitting down to feast on the pizzas you made. Sample local olive oil and limoncello and learn how to make authentic Italian pizza. Round-trip transportation is provided for this tour. Enjoy a meal of the pizza you made.

Sample Menu:

The main dish is pizza made of pizza dough. You will make your pizza lunch with the freshest ingredients.

What's Included:
Lunch
Air-conditioned vehicle and transportation

Holidays spent cooking at Villa Maria (Ravello):

Cooking Class: Guests can learn how to prepare local delicacies during cooking vacations offered by Villa Maria in Ravello. A guided walk of the villa's garden to select fresh produce is a standard part of the classes.

Market Visit: Before returning to the villa for the cooking class, take a guided market tour to choose your ingredients.

Mamma Agata's Cooking School (Ravello):

Cooking Class: Join a renowned cooking school in Ravello led by Mamma Agata. Learn to prepare traditional Amalfi Coast dishes in a family setting with a panoramic view.

Market Visit: Mamma Agata often starts her classes with a visit to the local markets to select fresh, seasonal ingredients.

Fresh Ingredients

CHAPTER 6: PRACTICALITIES AND RESOURCES

TRANSPORTATION TIPS

GETTING AROUND BY BUS, BOAT, AND CAR

How to Navigate the Amalfi Coast by Car:

S163, often known as "Amalfi Drive," is a single-lane road frequently congested. Given the traffic and the continuous turns, we advise driving with extreme caution.

Avoid traveling during rush hours, particularly in the summer, when the intense heat often causes traffic to stop completely. From May to the beginning of October, Saturdays and Sundays see exceptionally high visitation.

The scarcity of parking spaces along the Amalfi Coast is another issue. Finding parking in such small, steep settlements can be a significant challenge because the towns are pretty steep, plunging down the cliffside like life-sized Nativity scenes clinging to the mountainside.

While there are plenty of public and private parking lots in the towns, parking can cost up to €10 per hour.

Getting Around on a Scooter and Motorcycle:

The most enjoyable way to traverse the Amalfi Coast is on a moped or motorcycle, allowing visitors to explore the area without worrying about where to park or getting stuck in traffic.

In most of the Amalfi Coast villages, mopeds are available for rent. Naturally, we advise using a motorcycle or scooter to go around the Amalfi Coast only if you have a great deal of experience and are comfortable handling the numerous kilometers of sharp turns.

Using Amalfi Coast Public Transportation to Get Around:

All Amalfi Coast towns are accessible by the Sita bus company buses. Buses travel often. However, they frequently need to catch up due to the intensity of traffic on the SS163.

A seat on a bus packed with local vacationers traveling to the sea may only sometimes be available during the busiest times of the summer, so be prepared for the crowds. There can be occasions when you must ride standing up, and the driver will not let other passengers board.

If you take a Sita bus, you must purchase your tickets before boarding. Most taverns and tobacco shops along the Amalfi Coast sell tickets, which staff must verify on the bus.

It is not possible to buy tickets on board.

You must take a taxi if you wish to travel from one town to another in the evening without your car because buses do not operate at night.

Ferries:

Pros of Amalfi Coast Ferries: You can escape the traffic and enjoy panoramic views.

Cons: Only operates from April to October and is more costly than buses.

Every town along the coast is served by the Travelmar service, including smaller communities like Cetara, Minori, and Praiano. Their comparatively modest open-air boats give you a fantastic coastline view, and they operate starting on April 1. Ticket prices vary based on distance, from €5 to €15.

NLG offers direct ferries from Positano and Amalfi and from Salerno to Positano. In addition, Positano Jet provides circulation between the three principal hubs. Positano Jet costs between €15 and €20 for a one-way ticket, making it marginally more costly but marginally faster.

PARKING AND DRIVING ADVICE:

1. Choose a small car for narrow roads.
2. Drive during off-peak hours to avoid traffic.
3. Park outside city centers and use public transportation.
4. Look for parking garages in larger towns.
5. Be cautious of street parking regulations.

TRANSPORTATION TIPS:

1. Some hotels and restaurants offer valet parking.
2. Use parking apps to find available spaces.
3. Drive patiently and responsibly due to winding roads.
4. Plan your route efficiently.
5. Consider hiring a local driver for convenience.

SAFETY AND HEALTH

EMERGENCY CONTACTS:

National numbers
Carabinieri: 112
Emergency (police): 113
Firemen: 115
Car emergency (ACI): 116
Guardia di Finanza: 117
Health emergency: 118
Fire emergency: 1515
Sea emergency: 1530

Local numbers:
Health Guards: +39 089.854042
Info Office: +39 089.261484
P.zza S. Francesco, 15 Municipality Palace: +39 089.261068
C.so Umberto I, 47

EMERGENCY CONTACTS:
Municipality Police: +39 089.261381
Provincial Tourism Office: +39 089.857657
Post Office: +39 089.261065

Services:
Chemist Conte
C.so Umberto I, 43 - Ph. +39 089.261082 Bank CA.RI.ME

C.so V. Emanuele, 9 - Ph. +39 089.877387

HEALTH SERVICES

The Amalfi Coast offers public and private healthcare facilities with excellent quality treatment. The area is home to several clinics, hospitals, and pharmacies for the benefit of both residents and visitors. The Servizio Sanitario Nazionale (SSN), the nation's health system, provides free or inexpensive services to locals and nationals of the European Union in the context of public healthcare. Travel insurance may be required for non-EU visitors to cover medical costs. Although most medical personnel are professionally qualified, language could be problematic because not all healthcare providers speak English effectively. Ambulance services are available in case of emergencies and more serious.

Transporting patients to more extensive facilities in neighboring cities like Salerno or Naples might be necessary. Overall, the Amalfi Coast's medical facilities are dependable and effective. Still, according to a member who visited the Italian region, we advise getting travel insurance and being ready for any language barriers.

PHARMACIES:

Farmacia Elifani:

Monday-Saturday Hours: 8:30 a.m. - 1:30 p.m., 3:30 p.m. - 8:30 p.m.
Closed Sunday's
Get Directions

Via Angelo Cosenza 2 80062 Meta Italy
Website: farmaciaelifani.net
PH:081 8786605

Farmacia Napolitano Angelo:

Monday-Saturday Hours: 8:15 a.m.-1:00 p.m. and 4:00 p.m.-8:30 p.m.
Closed Sunday
Get Directions
Via Annunziatella 20 80042 Boscotrecase Italy
Website: farmacianapolitano.it
PH: 081 8581062

TRAVEL INSURANCE RECOMMENDATIONS

Why is having travel insurance necessary?

Travel insurance is crucial because it shields you from unforeseen expenses brought on by mishaps while on vacation.

Uncontrollable events have the potential to ruin your vacation plans and leave you severely broke. When traveling overseas, medical expenses alone can total thousands of dollars.

In perspective, the expense of receiving medical attention for a stomach virus in the USA and returning to the UK may reach £100,000. You would be responsible for paying those expenses if you did not have travel insurance.

The correct travel insurance policy can provide peace of mind that you are covered while traveling for anything from medical care and repatriation to trip cancellation and misplaced or stolen luggage.

Protection Against Medical Emergencies:

Make sure that your travel insurance covers medical emergencies and costs. Hospitalization, physician visits, and emergency medical evacuation should all fall under this category.

Cancellation and Interruptions of Trips:

Seek insurance that offers coverage if unforeseeable events—such as illness, injury, or other emergencies—cause you to postpone or cancel your vacation.

Insurance Against Missed Connections and Travel Delays:

Select insurance that will pay for additional lodging costs brought on by unanticipated events like weather delays, missed connections, or delayed flights.

Luggage and Individual Items:

Ensure the policy covers loss, theft, or damage to your belongings and luggage, Which is crucial for safeguarding priceless belongings like electronics, passports, and other necessities.

Emergency Departures and Returns:

Make sure that your policy covers repatriation and emergency evacuation.; Which is essential if you require a transfer to a better medical institution or, in the event of a severe medical emergency, return home.

CONCLUSION

FINAL THOUGHTS ON THE AMALFI COAST EXPERIENCE

The Amalfi Coast offers a mesmerizing and captivating experience that skillfully combines exquisite food, ancient history, and scenic beauty. Here are some closing reflections on the trip to the Amalfi Coast:

GORGEOUS SCENERY

The striking coastal scenery creates a breathtaking vista with pastel-colored settlements perched on rocks. The views from the twisting roads are spectacular at every bend.

CULTURAL LEGACY

With its ancient churches, medieval villages, and stunning buildings, the Amalfi Coast is rich in history. You can experience the region's rich past by investigating the cultural heritage of locations such as Positano, Ravello, and Amalfi.

CULINARY PLEASURES

The Amalfi Coast's gastronomic exploration is a sensory delight. The cuisine here showcases the area's bounty, with fresh seafood and homemade pasta with the well-known Limoncello liquor.

CHARMING TOWNS

Every coastal village has a distinct charm and personality. Every location offers a unique experience, whether it is Amalfi's vibrant alleys, Ravello's creative atmosphere, or Positano's seductive charm.

KIND HOSPITALITY

The folks' friendliness and kindness make a significant difference in the whole experience. Travelers frequently experience a warm welcome, which gives their experience a more intimate feel.

HIKING TRAILS AND HIDDEN GEMS

Going off the beaten road offers hiking trails that provide an alternative viewpoint of the shoreline and hidden gems. You can have a closer, more personal relationship with the natural environment by exploring the more sedate areas.

Concisely, the Amalfi Coast is an immersive experience that appeals to all senses, not just travelers. The Amalfi Coast creates an enduring impression for those fortunate enough to discover its treasures, thanks to its breathtaking scenery, mouthwatering food, and vibrant culture.

Blue Grotto

REFERENCES

REFERENCES

L ive Salerno. (n.d.). Amalfi Cathedral. Retrieved from https://w ww.livesalerno.com/amalfi-cathedral#google_vignette

Positano.com. (n.d.). Furore. Retrieved from https://www.po sitano.com/en/e/furore

Positano.com. (n.d.). The Best Time of Year to Visit the Amalfi Coast. Retrieved from https://www.positano.com/en/e/when-to-visit-the- amalfi-coast

Ravello.com. (n.d.). Villa Rufolo, Ravello - Amalfi Coast, Italy. Retrieved from https://www.ravello.com/attractions/villa-rufolo/

Travel Amalfi Coast. (n.d.). 10 Typical Dishes to Eat on the Amalfi Coast and Where to Do It. Retrieved from https://travelamalficoast.travelm ar.it/en/10-typical-dishes-to-eat-on-the-amalfi-coast-and-where-to- do-it

Trip.com. (n.d.). Amalfi Coast: Small group Market tour & Cooking Class in Praiano. Retrieved from https://www.trip.com/things-to-do/detail/17465173/

TourScanner. (n.d.). Boat Trips and Tours in Amalfi Coast. Retrieved from https://tourscanner.com/s/amalfi-coast/i/boat-tours/?campaign=10766787985&group=107822517244&keyword=boat%20tours%20amalfi%20coast&position=&target=kwd-934659193360&gclid=CjwKCAiAzJOtBhALEiwAtwj8tnj9hJSxpPEehyYNKfarrRXcjWSBB-DS_1CQFQCXfWU7SUOEqmQFhoCRE4Q

Viator. (n.d.). Amalfi Coast Kayak Tour along Arches, Beaches, and Sea Caves. Retrieved from Viator

Viator. (n.d.). Top Amalfi Coast Snorkeling. Retrieved from https://www.viator.com/Amalfi-Coast-tours/Snorkeling/d946-g17-c58

Walks of Italy. (2023, July 5). How To Get to the Amalfi Coast From Rome, Naples, & Beyond. Retrieved from https://www.walksofitaly.com/blog/travel-tips/how-to-get-to-amalfi-sorrento

WineTourism.com. (n.d.). Wineries Near Amalfi. Retrieved from WineTourism

Yelp. (n.d.). The Best 10 Pharmacy near Amalfi, Salerno, Italy. Retrieved from www.yelp.com.

About the Author

Wanderlust Wren, a dynamic 37-year-old flight attendant and travel enthusiast, is fueled by a profound passion for exploring the world and sharing her experiences through captivating travel books.

With a background in aviation and a natural wanderlust, Ms. Wren has dedicated her life to uncovering diverse destinations' hidden gems and cultural nuances. Her journey began as a 21-year-old flight attendant, weaving through bustling markets in Spain, navigating the serene landscapes of Hawaii, and immersing herself in the variety of wines and limoncello of Italy.

Drawing from years of globetrotting, Ms. Wren is not just a travel writer but a storyteller. Her narratives seamlessly blend adventure, cultural insights, and practical tips, making her books informative and a delightful reading experience. She believes in the transformative power of travel and strives to inspire readers to embark on their journeys of discovery.

Ms. Wren's travel books are more than just itineraries; they are windows into the heart of each destination through the eyes of a flight attendant. Her writing transcends the mundane, offering readers a vicarious adventure and encouraging them to step out of their comfort zones.

In the ever-changing travel landscape, Wanderlust Wren stands as a beacon, guiding readers with her infectious enthusiasm for exploration. Her mission is clear – to make the world more accessible to everyone, ignite the spirit of wanderlust, and showcase that travel's beauty lies not only in the destinations but also in the personal growth it fosters.

Embark on a journey with Wanderlust Wren, where every page is an invitation to discover, explore, and embrace the richness of our diverse world.

You can connect with me on:
🌐 https://wanderlust-wren.com

Subscribe to my newsletter:
✉ https://wanderlust-wren.com

Made in the USA
Las Vegas, NV
17 December 2024

14367598R00069